1

Hi, I'm Jason King. I come from Baryulgil in northern NSW - Bundjalung country. I'm an artist. I tell stories through my art.

Knowledge Books and Software

This is the Little Knowledge Warrior.
I painted this painting for my
grandson. It has some important
messages.

Knowledge Books and Software

This little warrior will learn many things in life, just like my grandson. This knowledge will make him strong and wise.

Knowledge Books and Software

I often paint animals in my paintings. Can you see one? Many Aboriginal people have an animal as their totem.

Knowledge Books and Software

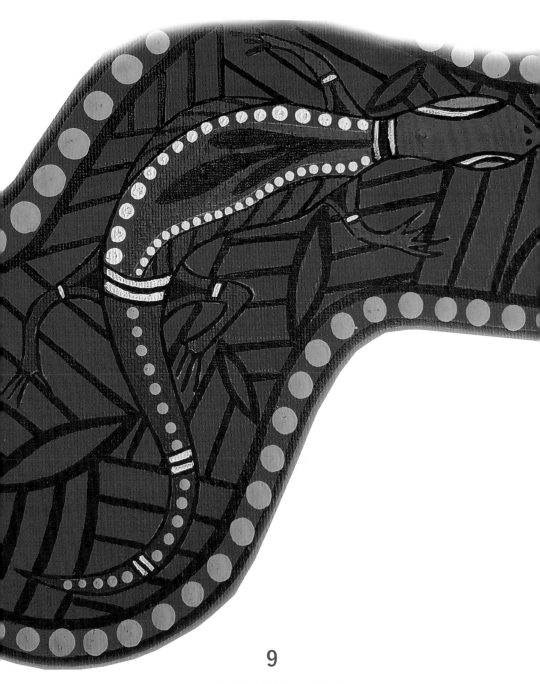

9

Totems are important. They are looked after and never hunted or eaten. They are protected by our people.

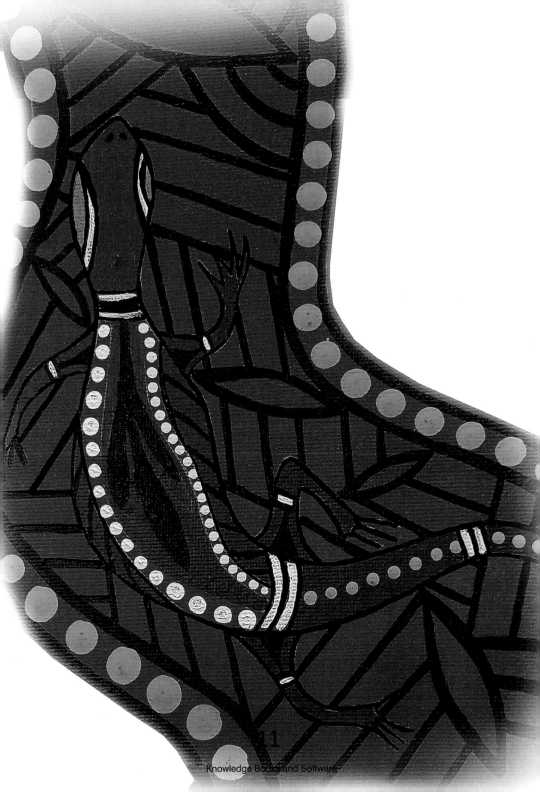

11

Can you see some lines with blue dots? They are time-lines. They show the long time between our ancestors and our people today.

Knowledge Books and Software

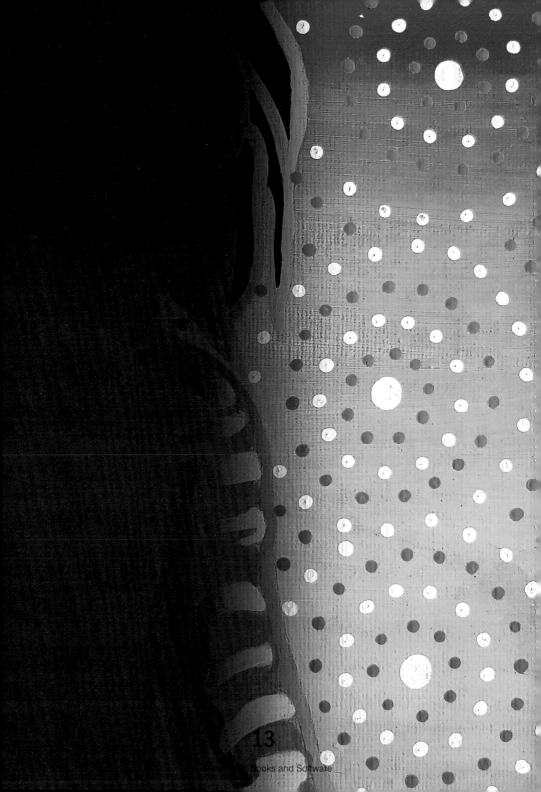

13

Our knowledge is passed down from our ancestors to us through these time-lines. Our stories and knowledge are kept alive this way.

Knowledge Books and Software

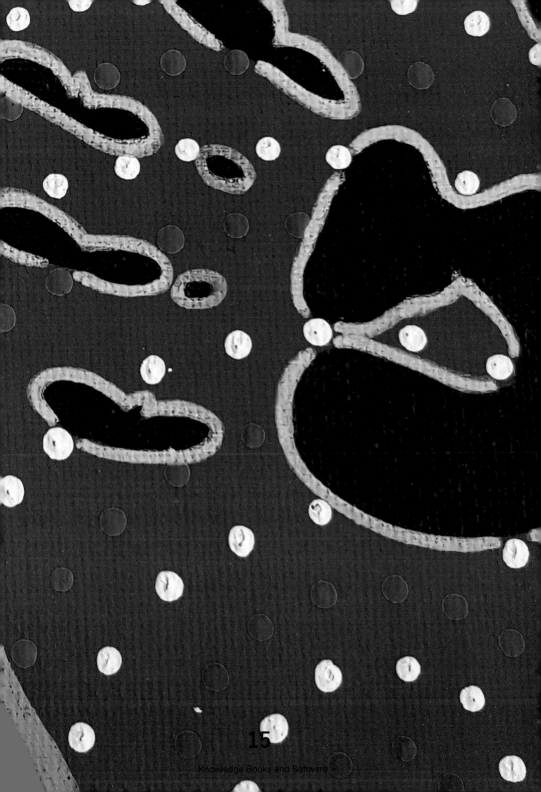

Knowledge Books and Software

Can you see some hand-prints?
They are the young people of today.
Without them, our stories would not
survive.

Knowledge Books and Software

We pass our stories on to our younger people. They can then share them with their children, and so on. This is called the cycle of life.

Knowledge Books and Software

Do you see a blank area above the little warrior's head? This is what would happen if we did not share our stories. Our knowledge would be lost forever.

Knowledge Books and Software

21

The Little Knowledge Warrior has a very important role. He is always learning and sharing his knowledge through stories and art. He helps to keep our culture alive. You can help him do this too!

23

Word bank

Baryulgil

Bundjalung

knowledge

warrior

important

messages

Aboriginal

totem

protected

time-lines

ancestors

survive

cycle

culture